In this series –

RUMI READINGS
FOR
ACHIEVEMENT

RUMI READINGS
FOR
ACHIEVEMENT

JALALUDDIN RUMI

The Scheherazade Foundation

The Scheherazade Foundation CIC
85 Great Portland Street
London
W1W 7LT
United Kingdom
www.SF.Charity
info@SF.Charity

First published by The Scheherazade Foundation CIC, 2025

RUMI READINGS FOR ACHIEVEMENT

© The Scheherazade Foundation

A CIP catalogue record for this title is available from the British Library.

ISBN 978-1-915311-68-9

Introduction

Jalaluddin Rumi was born in Balkh, Afghanistan, in the year 1207, and died in Konya, Turkey, in 1273.

During the sixty-six years spanning this pair of dates, he produced a range of extraordinary work in Persian which, today, is classed as 'Sufi Mysticism'.

In the seven and a half centuries since his death, Rumi's corpus, which includes *The Masnavi* and *Fihi Ma Fihi*, has been circulated widely across the Near East, the Arab world, and Central Asia.

Generations of students continue to commit selections of the 60,000 verses to heart, and allow Rumi's way of thought to permeate through all areas of their lives.

Although Orientalists venturing eastward from Europe in the 1700s occasionally made note of Sufi Mysticism, they tended to witness it through the more theatrical frills – such as 'whirling dervishes' – rather than through a deep appreciation of the texts.

It wasn't until the close of the nineteenth century that the first wholescale translations of Rumi's written work began to appear in Europe.

Even then, they remained very much the purview of a few academics, whose translations were – even for the time – laden with indescribably floral and cumbersome prose.

Although in the Occident, students would find themselves scrutinizing Rumi's corpus, it wasn't until more recently that accessible appreciations of his work became available.

A few years before his death, I asked my father – the Sufi scholar and thinker Idries Shah – for his thoughts on Rumi's legacy in the West.

Sitting in his favourite chair, a porcelain cup of green tea in hand, he looked at me hard.

'I never cease to be amazed,' he said.

'Amazed by what?'

'By the way people don't take what's perfectly packaged, and ready and waiting for them, but rather obsess with something else.'

'With what?'

'With endless and nonsensical trimmings, trappings, and paraphernalia.'

My father sipped his tea.

After a moment of silent thought, he continued:

'Read Rumi in the original Persian,' he said, 'and so delicate are the verses that you have tears rolling down your cheeks. Yet here in the West, it's served up as something submerged in a thick, glutinous gravy, so much so that its utterly inedible.'

I reminded my father that a series of publications had recently found their way to press – publications that presented Rumi's couplets in an utterly new way.

Stripped bare of what my father had referred to as 'gravy', they were light.

Indeed, they were lighter than light.

My father rolled his eyes at the thought.

'In any other place, and at any other time,' he said, 'people would be up in arms. Or, if they weren't, they'd be laughing until their sides split. Imagine it – Western poets with absolutely no knowledge of the original Persian text touting new, bestselling editions of Rumi's work! It's what we call "The Soup of the Soup of the Soup".'

In the years since my father's death, Occidental society has been flooded with all things Rumi.

Couplets ascribed to him are read solemnly at weddings across the United States, Europe, and beyond.

Wisdom drawn from his poetry is tattooed daily over the backs and limbs of Hollywood A-listers.

But the precious words uttered at weddings, tattooed into skin, and quoted in abundance, hold little or no bearing to the original verses of Jalaluddin Rumi.

So, there it is…

The great Sufi Master's wisdom available:

(a) in a form that's unreadable because it's all covered in glutinous gravy, or

(b) in another form that's completely distorted – the Soup of the Soup of the Soup.

One thing that *is* evident is that the West can benefit enormously from a clean, clear rendition of Rumi's thinking – as the East has done over the last seven hundred years.

For this reason, we have commissioned entirely new translations, gleaned in particular from *The Masnavi*. Selected and translated by native Persian-speaking scholars, the emphasis has been on maintaining the lightness of Rumi's poetry.

In an age of relentless speed and digital overload, and so as to allow the work to be accessed by those who may benefit from it most, we have arranged a series of bite-sized morsels by way of theme.

We encourage you to do what students, scholars, and ordinary people have done across the East for centuries…

To pick a single couplet, or a handful – and to read them over and over, allowing them to seed themselves in your mind.

Little by little, having taken root, they will blossom and bear fruit.

Tahir Shah

How to Use This Book

Rumi Readings for Achievement

You want to build something.

To move forward.

To do it well – maybe even beautifully.

And somewhere, beneath all of that, you want to become more fully yourself.

That's what this book is here for.

Rumi Readings for Achievement is not just about ambition or success. It's about what happens underneath and within the pursuit – the restlessness, the self-doubt, the breakthroughs, the late-night questions. It's about the *inner experience* of trying to grow, create, or accomplish something meaningful.

Each quote in this book has been selected from fresh translations of Rumi's original Persian texts. They are arranged to guide you through a quiet arc: from longing and preparation, through struggle, clarity, effort, and ultimately toward inner freedom – the kind of freedom that doesn't depend on outcomes.

You can read these words as inspiration, as wisdom, or as companionship. Some will energize you. Some will challenge you. Others may calm the part of you that thinks you need to do more, faster, better.

Let each quote be a pause, not a push.

Let it reconnect you to what really matters.

A Steady Companion for Your Journey

You don't need to read this book all at once. In fact, we recommend the opposite.

Keep it nearby – on your desk, in your bag, at your bedside. Open it when you feel discouraged. Or determined. Or unsure. Or proud. Let it meet you in all the phases of your striving.

There are ten sections in this book, each exploring a different dimension of achievement – from preparation and persistence, to overcoming fear, to staying grounded in the midst of pressure.

You can follow the sequence, or open anywhere. However you move through it, trust that the right quote will find you when it's needed.

One Quote at a Time

Try reading a single quote each morning – before the meetings, the emails, the tasks begin. Or in the evening, when you need to let go of what didn't get done.

Read it slowly. Let it echo a little.
Then ask yourself:

- What part of me is this speaking to?
- What if I believed this today?

You may want to keep a notebook nearby. Write down a line that stays with you. Add your own thoughts, questions, dreams.

Let the Words Work Quietly

Achievement can become noisy. Loud expectations. Internal pressure. Constant measuring.

This book is a counterpoint.

It reminds you that stillness can be powerful.

That rest is not weakness.

That there is a part of you already whole, already wise – even as you strive to become more.

Let the quotes work in the background. Don't force them to 'inspire' you. Some may not speak to you right away. That's okay. Others may become companions for months or years to come.

Not Every Step Is Forward

Rumi knew what it meant to get stuck. To fall apart. To long for more and not know how to reach it.

That's part of why his voice remains so alive – because he doesn't just celebrate the destination.

He meets you in the in-between.

So if you find yourself doubting, circling, or burning out, this book is still for you. Especially for you.

These words are reminders that the inward journey matters just as much – perhaps more – than what the world sees.

Share the Wisdom

You might find that a quote stays with you so clearly that you want to share it – with a colleague, a friend, a student, or a team. Do.

Sometimes, the most powerful thing you can bring into a high-pressure environment is a line of poetry. It doesn't need to be explained. Just spoken.

Read it aloud in a meeting. Write it on a Post-it. Offer it without commentary.

You might be surprised at the way it lands.

Let This Be Enough

In the end, this book is not asking you to change everything. It's not adding another task to your list.

It is here to remind you of what you already carry – the spark, the calling, the dignity of trying.

Rumi writes: '*Go beyond thought as you would go beyond the limits of Fate, and progress, progress.*'

Let your work be guided not only by thought, but by something deeper – a longing, a clarity, a truth. Progress is not only forward – it is inward.

Part 1

Ways of Achieving Success

1

He has fine aesthetic sense
and deep appreciation for beauty.
How can a young man choose an old crone
over a woman his own age?
Positive qualities attract more positive qualities;
negative qualities do not.
Recite to him the verse:
'The pure are destined
for the pure.'

2

When you close your eyes,
sadness wraps itself around you.
How can the distant radiance of the eye be seen?
If you feel sorrow, even while fully aware,
know that the innermost core of your being,
the seat of intuition
and understanding,
is asleep.
Wake it up!

3

How strange!
When will I have the chance to see my own reflection?
Do I possess the wisdom of daylight?
Or do I carry the ignorance of darkness?
I asked about the purpose of a mirror:
it is to reveal identity, and nature.

4

The mirror of the soul reflects only
the face of the beloved,
the face of the beloved hailing from
the same land.

5

I urged my own heart:
'Strive to find that magnificent reflection,
turn your eyes towards the vast ocean;
the stream alone is not enough.'

6

To be considered worthy,
you must fully engage with the spirit.
If you mix with those drunk on passion,
then you, too, will be no more than a drunk.
Thoughts both guide and attract,
pulling you toward a particular destination.
Go beyond thought
as you would go beyond the limits of Fate,
and progress, progress.

7

He who crosses the facade of imitation
perceives all things illuminated by Truth.
This glimmering light, beyond logic or language,
penetrates the surface and reaches within.

8

Adam's fall was born of his passion and yearning,
while Iblis's[1] downfall came from pride and arrogance.

---

1   The leader of the devils, in Islamic tradition.

9

The truly intelligent possess real manners,
as their hearts are attuned to hidden truths.

10

The soul rises up on wings,
while the body clings to the ground below.

Part 2

Traits of a Successful Person

11

Those who have reached their destination
no longer need a guide,
having found peace and understanding in their journey.
It is essential that these travellers then offer guidance
while everyone else remains at the start.

12

Strive to attain profound
knowledge and unwavering belief
to grasp the true essence of things,
like all-enveloping wisdom.

13

Though you may appear just a tiny thing,
your true nature encompasses
the entire universe.

14

When a wise and articulate leader emerges,
the concept of duality fades
and unity takes its place.
As falcons, quarreling and discordant,
come to perceive the call of the falconer:
the disputes cease.
Change your focus from disagreement to unity,
and find joy as you come together from all directions.

15

The heart that radiates with the glow of moonlight
offers countless opportunities to the mystic.
With you, there is an impenetrable barrier;
with them, there is an open door.
With you, I find indifference;
with the beloved, I am cherished.

16

According to the Prophet,
all prophets, including Adam, are his disciples,
adhering to the principles of Truth.
He revealed the mystery with his statement:
'We are the last, yet the most distinguished.'

17

With every breath, they experience a unique elevation,
as God bestows a singular crown upon their heads.
They may physically dwell on this Earth,
but their essence resides in a realm
that transcends human understanding,
a domain beyond the grasp of those
who seek to comprehend it.

18

The saints possess extraordinary abilities,
having the power to redirect an arrow, once shot,
back along its original path.

19

The spiritual master,
like God,
operates without the need for physical tools,
imparting wisdom to his followers
through silent means.
He has the ability to effortlessly mould hearts,
shaping them like pliable wax.
His love can turn dishonour into respect,
and respect into humiliation.
This affection is visibly marked,
like a wax seal
which serves as a clear testament to the truth.

20

He possesses a luminous quality, like light,
with Gabriel representing his great intellect.
The lower saint serves as his guiding light,
from which we discover our own unique position.
The Divine illumination encompasses various degrees.
The light of Truth is obscured by seven hundred layers,
each representing different levels of brightness.
Each veil conceals a distinct group,
all converging towards the Imam.

Part 3

Examining the Qualities of Successful People

21

Without the need for words,
I communicate with you in a different way,
revealing ancient mysteries.
Pay attention!

22

The elusive essence of the heart's highest point
is the royal path,
an illuminating radiance that transcends
geographical limitations,
emanates from a magnificent source.

23

He is entirely annihilated
in the qualities of the Divine.
Yet within this annihilation
his true existence survives.

24

The pains of illness and fever are regarded as beneficial,
and the discomforts and sicknesses experienced
at night are seen as a blessing.

25

The state of pure awe emerges from formlessness,
generating a multitude of manifestations,
without need for instruments or tools.
The abstract force of formlessness
skillfully constructs new hands,
while the essence of the individual moulds
the physical appearance of humanity.

26

Anything that once had indications loses its significance,
while that which lacks indications gains fame.

27

Those who lose sense of self
encompass everyone,
while a friend encompasses all friends
by not being a friend themselves.

28

Inspect your 'poverty' twice a day
to perceive genuine riches in supposed want.

29

Mortality is accepted as the door to immortality:
a falling leaf is cherished as a blessing.

30

I received both the message of Truth and its greeting
from a person of refinement.
This salutation, which brings me more joy than any scent,
encapsulates the very essence of everything I cherish.

Part 4

Skills Necessary for Success

31

When choosing a teacher,
evaluate the condition and qualities of their experience,
and select the one who best embodies
the true attributes of a genuine guide.

32

The speech of intellect,
even if it concerns pearls and corals,
differs from the discourse of the soul.
Talk of the soul belongs to a different realm;
its fundamental nature requires
other foundation.
Intellectual and sensory dialogues can be either outcomes
or causes of phenomena,
while the discourse of the soul is either extraordinary
or incomprehensible.
The illumination of the soul is fleeting;
the necessary and sufficient conditions
do not always align.

33

He said:
Truth grants you power and control.
Your leadership will endure indefinitely;
your stewardship will remain steadfast.

34

The one who possesses a true heart
acts as a mirror in all six directions,
while the Divine sees through them
in all six dimensions.

35

Those who have attained unity
reflect their inner state and expression.
Their lips remain closed
while their eyes, detached from worldly sights,
reveal the beauty they experience within.

36

The Sheikh perceived the individual's thoughts.
For the Sheikh, like a lion,
makes hearts his domain to rule over.

37

The skies dutifully serve his moon;

both East and West depend on his provision.

Without you, *Lawlak*[2] would remain bound by His decree,

ensuring sustenance and provision for all.

Without him, the skies would lack all movement, light,

place, and dominion.

---

2 Referring to the *Hadith*: 'Without you (O Muhammad) I would not have created creation.'

38

The person of good character
is one who, with humility,
is patient with the angry and unkind.

39

God, grant abundance to those who are generous
(and bring destruction upon the miserly),
but especially upon the magnanimous ones
who selflessly give their lives,
offering their own throats in sacrifice to You.

40

Have faith in God and remain steadfast;
let neither fear nor hesitation sway your actions.
Your means of livelihood is more devoted to you
than you are to it.
Love is actively pursuing you;
impatience reveals nothing, you fool.

Part 5

Characteristics of the Path to Success

41

Storm the heavens without wings or feathers,
like the sun, and the full and crescent moons.
When you are in spirit, not in body,
you need not consume a hundred morsels of food.
The whale of sorrow does not sink your ship,
nor does the ugliness of death trouble you.

42

Return to the mine once more
and extract only pure gold
to cleanse your hands of impurities.

43

Abraham chose not to escape
from the impending disaster,
and instead stayed behind.
This decision led to him abandoning his
reputation and facing rejection.
It is strange that while one object does not catch fire,
another one does.
The quest is like an inverted horseshoe.

44

Due to their lack of knowledge of the way,
they lead as if they were ignorant,
relying solely on trust,
like a blind person relying on the sound of footsteps.
Trust alone in times of conflict is like depending
on chance in a game of dice.

45

Understanding this allows for great progress,
as the realm of God's creation is vast
and within our reach.
While this state of enlightenment
may seem like a mere beginning,
there exists a higher significance
within the sacred domain.

46

When your life is overwhelmed
by a sense of shame and dishonour,
the act of reciting *A'udhu* and *Fatiha*[3] loses its appeal.
Though Haneen's sobbing may seem devoid of emotion,
negligence, which lacks any emotional response,
is even more certain.

---

3   Passages from the Qur'an.

47

The wolf often captures its victim
when the lamb is alone.
Within the flock, a young lamb stands apart.
One who abandons tradition for the sake of company
within such a lair, who does not spill their own blood?
Tradition serves as a guiding path,
while the group functions as a companion.
Without clear direction and someone to accompany you,
you are likely to encounter danger.

48

When something persists for an extended time,
it is sometimes seen as the fruit of boredom.
Was it the victim of its own actions,
or merely deceptive perception?
It is good to engage in physical exercise for one hour
and replenish energies by seeking comfort.
When contraction takes place,
observe an expansion within it.
Remain alert, and avoid furrowing your brow.

49

Like a reclusive mystic
who remains undisturbed on their journey,
peacefully traversing countless realms.
If such behaviour were not guided by a higher hand,
where would accounts of that land come from?
These authentic narratives
have been corroborated by the consensus
of hundreds of thousands of elders.

50

The pursuit of perfection is a profound,
compelling endeavour,
especially for those who hold
illusion within their souls.
Blood will flow abundantly from your heart and eyes
until you rid yourself of self-admiration.
The cause of Satan's downfall
was a false belief in his superiority,
and this condition resides within
the essence of every living being.

Part 6

The Standard of Attaining Success

51

Proximity eliminates the concept of spatial orientation,
making notions of left, right,
behind, and ahead irrelevant to the mind.
How can proximity exist without 'how' for the king?
The intellect is incapable of grasping it.

52

Proximity remains constant;
neither increasing nor decreasing.
Proximity to the Divine involves transcending
the perception of one's own existence.
For something that does not exist,
there is no concept of being above or below.
For something that does not exist,
there is no concept of time,
not in terms of proximity or distance,
nor in terms of 'early' or 'late'.

53

The souls of the Simurghs exist beyond Mount Qaf,[4]
and their nature is not easily comprehensible
to every mind.
Except for those who directly observe the occurrence,
a state of disconnection follows the witnessing of it.

---

4   A reference to the imagery used in Attar's *Conference of the Birds*.

54

The essence lies in the inherent power of attraction.
But, dear companion,
be diligent and place your trust in that very attraction.
Abandoning effort is pride,
and pride cannot coexist with self-sacrifice.

55

Unaware of events in the world,
both by day and at night,
like a pen guided by divine force.
Those who fail to recognize this influence
behind the written words mistakenly attribute the action
to the physical act of writing alone.

56

I assume the role of his vision, dexterity, and emotions in order to protect his wealth from mistaken direction.

57

The bride has made herself known
to both commoners and aristocrats,
yet spends her time exclusively with the monarch.
A large portion of Sufis are people
who live in the present moment,
yet those among them with enduring qualities are rare.

58

The challenge of comprehension
lies in the limitations of language,
and transient conditions.
Attempting to wash blood with blood
is both impractical and illogical.

59

Stay silent,
and allow the king to issue his command.
Do not offer the nightingale
this or that particular rose.
This rose is vibrant, brimming with intensity and urgency.
O nightingale, forsake words,
and become an attentive observer.

60

You should derive as much satisfaction
from the representation of friends
as from extracting water from the boundless sea.
By replicating the vision
it transforms into genuine
comprehension through repetition.
Do not separate from friends until
you have achieved understanding;
the formation of the pearl is not complete
until it emerges from the shell.

Part 7

The Impact of
Faith on Success

61

O, believer!
You have gained the ability
to perceive with divine illumination,
which shields you from error and mistake.

62

The letters *Mīm*, *Wāw*, *Mīm*, and *Nūn*[5] hold meaning
beyond being ordinary titles;
the term 'believer' carries a deeper meaning
than a simple label.

---

5   Often seen at the beginning of certain Qur'anic chapters.

63

The souls of wolves and dogs are distinct,
whereas the souls of God's lions are fused together.

64

When a believer looks at another who shares the same faith, their face remains free from impurities.

65

When the air is not fresh,
faith, too, loses its freshness.
The key to unlocking the door cannot be obtained
through desire alone.

66

On the Day of Judgement, a day filled with fear,
it will be a joyous occasion for the faithful
and a time of annihilation for beasts.
On the Day of Judgement,
the birds will resemble vessels adrift
on the vast expanse of water.

67

Miracles do not generate faith;
instead, they reveal attributes by their inherent nature.
Enemies are the recipients of miracles,
while the essence of religion is to unite hearts.

68

You possess qualities like those
found among the inhabitants of hell
who remain devout.
The act of extinguishing fire
is within the realm of possibility for them.
The destruction caused by the inferno
becomes illumination for the faithful,
as it is impossible to counteract a force
without its opposite.

69

Patience is the ultimate manifestation of faith;
without patience, faith cannot exist.
As the Prophet said,
Faith is not granted to those
who lack the virtue of patience.

70

A believer is someone
who remains steadfast in their faith
in both favourable and unfavourable circumstances.
While the unbeliever can only long
for such unwavering conviction.

Part 8

The Veils that Conceal Success

71

The rise of selfish desires
leads to the concealment of true art,
creating numerous barriers
from the eyes to the heart.

72

Just as the spider,
that repugnant creature, weaves its web,
forcefully removing decayed material
from its individual threads.
It creates a luminous barrier with its saliva
which impairs its vision and blinds it.

73

Like the pearl in the ocean
that asks where the sea is,
the illusion, like a shell, builds its own barrier.
The question 'Where is it?' is obscured by its cloak,
shrouding the brilliance of the sun.

74

The realm of illusion, fantasy, greed, and fear
is a significant obstacle for the traveller.
The intricate patterns created by this deception,
like a towering mountain before Khalil,
pose a danger.

75

Fools chase the shining sun.
In the barrenness of the desert,
a solitary candle glows.
The entire world is illuminated by its light.
How can it be made perceptible to the world?

76

Despite being blind,
he believes he can see;
what should remove the obstacle
often becomes the obstacle itself.

77

His perception is sharp in recognizing both
success and failure,
yet he focuses on tangible things
rather than subtle nuances.

78

These causes act as obstacles to clear perception,
as not every observation merits His skill.

79

No matter what you say or express,
you only add another layer of concealment.

80

The Light of Truth is obscured by seven hundred veils,
layers of light that cover one another.
Behind each veil lies a distinct group of people.
These veils are arranged in rows leading up to the Imam.

Part 9

The Role of Travel in Success

81

Travel is often seen as a way to explore the world, and evaluate one's fortune and means of living.

82

How can the moon achieve full illumination
or attain a status like that of King Kai Khosrow[6]
without movement?
Through the act of travelling,
the pawn becomes a queen,
and Joseph[7] discovers new aspirations.

---

6 A Sassanian 'King of Kings' of the 6th century C.E. also known as
   Anushirvan, 'the immortal soul'.
7 Joseph son of Jacob, of the Old Testament story.

83

My desire is closely linked to travel;
it is through travelling
that I may come to find it present within myself.

84

While travelling, you uttered these words:
'O God, bestow upon me the presence
of the chosen people.'
Oh Lord, grant my heart the discernment
to recognize those
who are dedicated, humble and sincere.

85

Remain silent,
but align yourself with the path of truth,
roaming, faltering in the pursuit of love.
This journey is the act of approaching God,
and our progress on the camel represents that voyage.

86

A solitary traveller may find joy on their journey,
but with companions
their experience becomes exponentially more fulfilling.

87

Though I may travel and explore distant lands,
how can my love for my homeland
ever fade from my heart?

88

The enjoyment and delights of home are often amplified
by the challenges faced during travel.
Once you have navigated unfamiliar territories
and encountered the beauty of settled life
and cherished companions,
the hardships of travel become a distant memory.

89

External travel pertains to our physical movements
and outward behaviour,
while internal travel signifies the spiritual journey
towards higher levels of enlightenment and transcendence.

90

The mystic's journey is swift compared
to the king's ascent to the throne,
while the ascetic's journey spans a full day
for each month.
Although the ascetic
might experience an extraordinary day,
a single day cannot compare to fifty thousand.

Part 10

The Function of a Mentor
in Attaining Success

91

Under the guidance of a knowledgeable mentor,
those who lack the ability to guide others
remain lost and aimless.
The mentor's presence may cast a shadow
as large as Mount Qaf,
yet their spirit soars gracefully like the majestic Simurgh.

92

O God! Please choose those
with strong character and integrity
to discern between truth and falsehood.
Those who are confined by deceptive illusions
can only find true wisdom in the prophets and messengers.

93

From among the ranks of the seemingly impoverished,
discern and select the one
who possesses genuine wisdom and insight.

94

The heart of a true guide unveils subtle miracles
and hidden wonders.
Within them lie countless insights and revelations,
the most remarkable of which is their closeness
to the divine.

95

According to the Sheikh,
true unity is achieved through the guidance
of a genuine mentor,
while the actions of the envious only lead to division.

96

The guide acts as a mirror,
reflecting the soul's deepest emotions
and revealing its true state.
Therefore, it is wise for the soul to refrain
from expressing its turmoil in the presence of this mirror.

97

When the heart experiences contentment,
see it as a reflection of the sun's ascent in the sign of Aries.
Spring and autumn both reveal their vibrant beauty
as flowers mingle with lush meadows.

98

With few exceptions,
people rarely go beyond their origins.

99

Those who possess genuine discernment in their speech
experience both delight and adversity as
inseparable companions.
Their outward demeanour instils
a sense of urgency in your journey,
but their behaviour undermines your resolve.

100

The influence and impact of a leader are far more
significant than merely acknowledging the truth;
true satisfaction and fulfilment surpass
even the finest of pleasures.

Finis

www.ingramcontent.com/pod-product-compliance
Lightning Source LLC
Chambersburg PA
CBHW020450100426
42813CB00031B/3312/J